Published by Grolier Books, a division of Grolier
Enterprises Inc.

Disney Presents The Wonderful World of Knowledge
ISBN 0-7172-8929-X
Birds ISBN 0-7172-8940-0

© 1999 Disney

First published in 1999

Printed and bound in China by
Toppan Printing Company

Originated in Italy by Articolor

Designed and compiled by
Marshall Editions Developments Limited

GROLIER
B O O K S

DISNEY PRESENTS

The Wonderful World of Knowledge

BIRDS

Using The Wonderful World of Knowledge

 **M**ickey, Minnie, Donald, Daisy, Goofy, and Pluto are ready to take you on an adventure ride through the world of learning. Discover the secrets of science, nature, our world, the past, and much more. Climb aboard and enjoy the ride.

Look here for a general summary of the theme

Labels tell *you what's happening in the pictures*

The pictures by *themselves can tell you a lot, even before you read a word*

Mickey's ears *lead you to one of the main topics*

Watch out for special pages where Mickey takes a close look at some key ideas

The Solar System

👉 The Solar System is the name given to our Sun and its family of planets. It also includes the planets' moons, millions of pieces of rock called asteroids and meteoroids, and frozen lumps of dust and gas called comets. Everything else you can see in the sky is outside the Solar System and is far, far away. Every single star is itself a sun, and each may have its own family of planets and moons.

Saturn is surrounded by beautiful rings

REPTILES AND AMPHIBIANS

Color and Camouflage

Frogs and toads come in nearly every imaginable color, even gold or black. They have a wide range of patterns, from spots and stripes to zigzags.

Color and pattern help frogs and toads survive. Bright colors warn that they may be poisonous. Drab colors camouflage them, or hide them against their background. Many tree frogs are exactly the same green as leaves, while others look like bark. The Asian horned toad has the best camouflage of all. Folds of patchy, brown skin and a flat body make it look like a dead leaf when it lies still on the forest floor.

Folds of brown skin give perfect camouflage

Flat body is hard to see among dead leaves

Asian horned toad

False-eyed frog

Markings look like eyes

For extra protection, bad-smelling liquid oozes out around false eyes

FALSE-EYED FROG
The South American false-eyed frog has large markings on its flanks that look like eyes. These fool some predators into thinking that they are looking at a much larger animal, such as a cat or bird.

COLOR AND CAMOUFLAGE

Dog sniffing curiously at the toad

Strawberry arrow frog

POISON-DART FROGS
Deadly poison oozes from the skin of Central and South American poison-dart frogs. People in the rain forest rub the tips of their arrows and blowpipe darts on the skin of these frogs to collect the poison to use for hunting.

Blue poison-dart frog

Oriental fire-bellied toad defending itself against a dog

Skin oozes a stinging fluid

Bright colored belly

Green and black back

FIRE-BELLIED TOAD
When cornered by a predator, the Oriental fire-bellied toad of eastern Asia arches its back and rears up on its legs to show its fiery underside. Wise attackers back off, because the toad's skin oozes a stinging, bad-tasting fluid.

Toad rears up on its back legs

16

17

FIND OUT MORE
MAMMALS: Camouflage
PLANET EARTH: Forests

Mickey's page *numbers help you look things up. Don't forget there's a glossary and index at the back of each book*

Goofy and his *friends know how to give you a chuckle on every topic*

Mickey points you to more information in other books in your *The Wonderful World of Knowledge*

 **FIND OUT MORE**
MAMMALS: Camouflage
PLANET EARTH: Forests

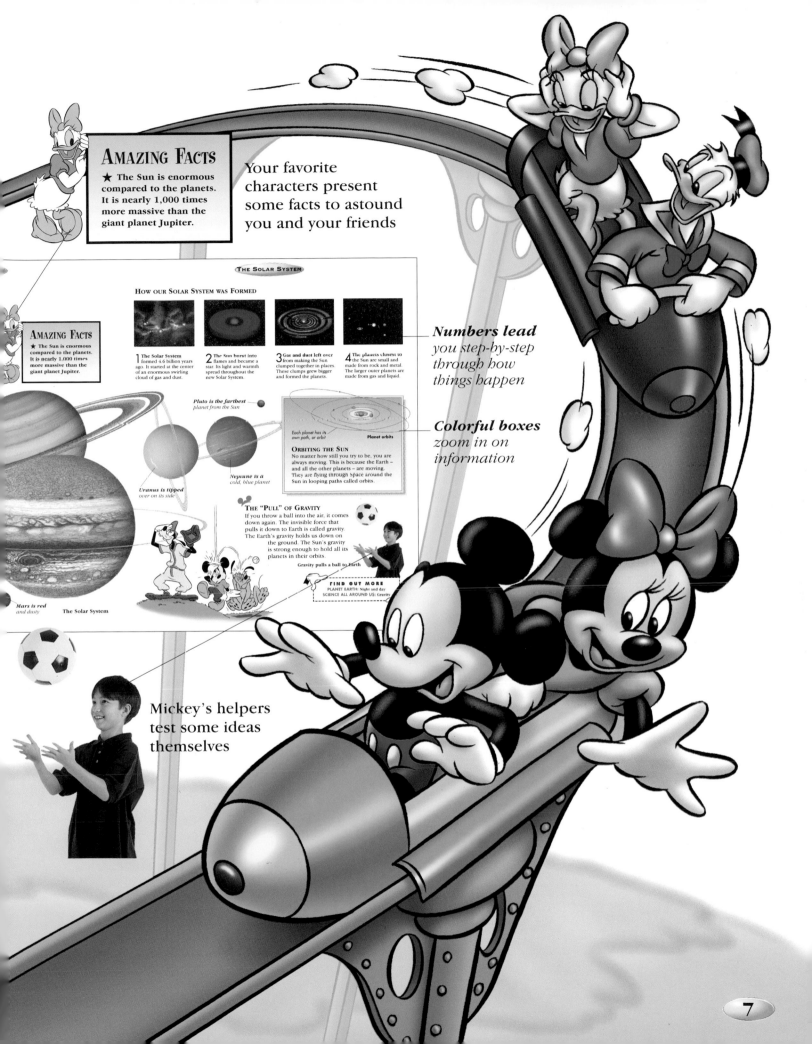

AMAZING FACTS

★ The Sun is enormous compared to the planets. It is nearly 1,000 times more massive than the giant planet Jupiter.

Your favorite characters present some facts to astound you and your friends

AMAZING FACTS

★ The Sun is enormous compared to the planets. It is nearly 1,000 times more massive than the giant planet Jupiter.

THE SOLAR SYSTEM

HOW OUR SOLAR SYSTEM WAS FORMED

1 The Solar System formed 4.6 billion years ago. It started at the center of an enormous swirling cloud of gas and dust.

2 The Sun burst into flames and became a star. Its light and warmth spread throughout the new Solar System.

3 Gas and dust left over from making the Sun clumped together in places. These clumps grew bigger and formed the planets.

4 The planets closest to the Sun are small and made from rock and metal. The larger outer planets are made from gas and liquid.

Numbers lead *you step-by-step through how things happen*

Pluto is the farthest planet from the Sun

Neptune is a cold, blue planet

Uranus is tipped over on its side

Each planet has its own path, or orbit

Planet orbits

Colorful boxes *zoom in on information*

ORBITING THE SUN

No matter how still you try to be, you are always moving. This is because the Earth – and all the other planets – are moving. They are flying through space around the Sun in looping paths called orbits.

THE "PULL" OF GRAVITY

If you throw a ball into the air, it comes down again. The invisible force that pulls it down to Earth is called gravity. The Earth's gravity holds us down on the ground. The Sun's gravity is strong enough to hold all its planets in their orbits.

Gravity pulls a ball to Earth

FIND OUT MORE
PLANET EARTH: Night and day
SCIENCE ALL AROUND US: Gravity

Mars is red and dusty   The Solar System

Mickey's helpers test some ideas themselves

Contents

INTRODUCING
Birds

All over the world, the sight of graceful wings and the chorus of birdsong is a pleasure. There are over 9,000 species of birds, from waders to songbirds, many of which have their own special habits and characteristics.

Birds live almost everywhere, in the air, on land, and in water. There are tiny hummingbirds and huge eagles. There are birds that cannot fly and birds that fly halfway around the world every year. These feathered creatures are some of nature's most amazing acrobats and treasured beauties.

Flightless Birds

Even though all the 9,000 or more species, or types, of birds in the world have wings, not all birds can fly. These flightless birds, such as the ostrich and emu, usually have small wings and long, powerful legs. Instead of flying, they can run fast to escape danger or find food. Most have long necks, too, which helps them spot enemies at a distance. The flightless kiwi is much smaller and is not a fast runner. It prefers to come out at night to feed.

SPEEDY OSTRICH

The world's tallest bird is the ostrich. It stands up to 2.7 m (9 ft) tall. It is also the fastest bird on the ground, running on its long legs at up to 70 km/h (43 mph). The ostrich lives in Africa and lays the largest egg of any bird. The egg weighs about 1.5 kg (3 lb).

Male ostriches in the African savanna

Tail feathers

Long legs *help the ostrich run fast over long distances*

Large foot *with strong toes*

Emu

AUSTRALIAN GIANT

At 2 m (7 ft) tall, the emu is the second tallest bird in the world. It has coarse, floppy feathers, which give it a shaggy look, and tiny wings. Emus run fast, traveling long distances in the desert lands of Australia to find grasses, seeds, and insects to eat.

BUSY PARENT

The rhea is South America's tallest bird, at 1.3 m (4 ft) tall. The male rhea mates with several females, looks after all the chicks that hatch, and shows them how to find food.

Male rhea with young

Large eye allows ostrich to see a long way

Long neck gives the ostrich a good view of the surroundings

Long, soft wing feathers – males flap their wings when courting females

An ostrich reaches down to peck plants, insects, and even reptiles, from the ground, but it regularly looks up to watch for danger

AMAZING FACTS

★ The ostrich's eye is bigger than the world's smallest bird, the bee hummingbird, which is 5.7 cm (2¼ in) long.

The cassowary has a blue neck

FOREST BIRD

The cassowary lives in the tropical forests of New Guinea and Australia. It has big, powerful legs and a hard crest, called a casque, on its head. The cassowary may use this casque to help break its way through the dense forest.

DIGGING FOR FOOD

The little kiwi of New Zealand has a long beak with nostrils at its tip. It has a good sense of smell and uses its beak to dig in the ground for worms and insects.

Kiwi

FIND OUT MORE
ATLAS OF THE WORLD: Australia
REPTILES AND AMPHIBIANS: Reptiles

Game Birds

In some countries there are birds that are hunted for food or sport. These birds are known as game birds. They can fly and they often roost, or settle for the night, in trees. There are over 260 different species in this group. It includes birds such as peacocks, with their glittering tails, grouse, turkeys, and pheasants. Most have heavy bodies with short, strong beaks and powerful legs for scratching in the ground for seeds and berries.

BOOMING CALL

Curassows live in the forests of South America. They find their food on the ground, but flutter up into trees if in danger. The male bird makes a low booming call to help him attract females in the dense forest.

Crest of curly feathers and a knob of yellow skin decorate the curassow's head

Male curassow

Twigs and leaves from the ground are used to make the curassow's nest up in trees

FAN OF FEATHERS

The male peacock has splendid long, colorful tail feathers, patterned with markings like glowing eyes. To impress the female peacock, the male lifts his feathers and spreads them like a glittering fan.

Male peacock's impressive display

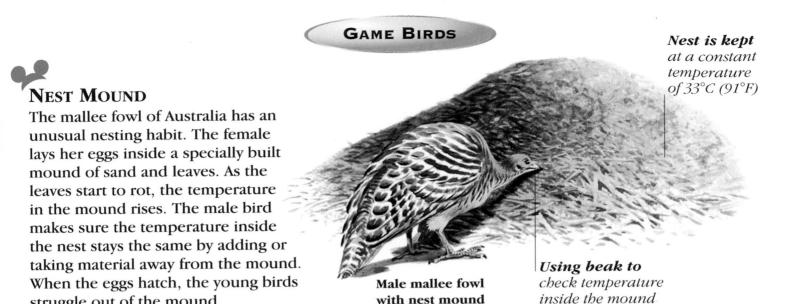

NEST MOUND

The mallee fowl of Australia has an unusual nesting habit. The female lays her eggs inside a specially built mound of sand and leaves. As the leaves start to rot, the temperature in the mound rises. The male bird makes sure the temperature inside the nest stays the same by adding or taking material away from the mound. When the eggs hatch, the young birds struggle out of the mound.

Nest is kept *at a constant temperature of 33°C (91°F)*

Using beak to *check temperature inside the mound*

Male mallee fowl with nest mound

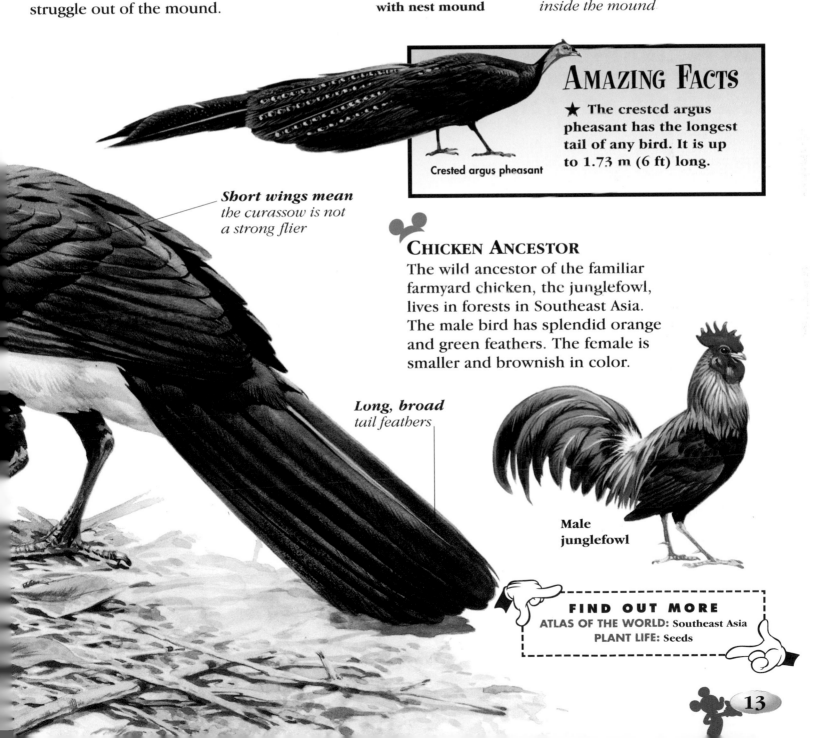

AMAZING FACTS

★ The crested argus pheasant has the longest tail of any bird. It is up to 1.73 m (6 ft) long.

Crested argus pheasant

Short wings mean *the curassow is not a strong flier*

CHICKEN ANCESTOR

The wild ancestor of the familiar farmyard chicken, the junglefowl, lives in forests in Southeast Asia. The male bird has splendid orange and green feathers. The female is smaller and brownish in color.

Long, broad *tail feathers*

Male junglefowl

FIND OUT MORE
ATLAS OF THE WORLD: Southeast Asia
PLANT LIFE: Seeds

Ground-feeding Birds

Birds such as cranes, rails, and bustards do fly, but prefer to spend most of their time on the ground, eating grain, insects, and small animals. They nest on or close to the ground, too. Some rails, and their relative the sunbittern, also search for food on marshland, or wade into shallow streams. Most of these birds have long legs, and cranes are among the tallest of all flying birds, at up to 1.5 m (5 ft) tall.

CRANE DISPLAY
All cranes perform display dances when courting mates. The birds stretch out their wings to show off their feathers. They strut about, bobbing their heads up and down, and jump into the air from time to time.

Wings outstretched
to display feathers

Crest of yellow
feathers on crowned
crane's head

**Water rail feeding on
small water creatures**

Cranes stay
with the same
mate for life

SHY WATER BIRD
The shy water rail lurks among reeds, searching for food, such as insects and frogs, with its long red beak. It swims well and also catches fish and other small water creatures. Its neat cup-shaped nest is usually made on the ground among rushes.

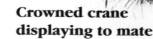

**Crowned crane
displaying to mate**

Head is patterned
red, white, and black

Crane flies
with its legs
and neck
stretched out

...ned crane in flight

AMAZING FACTS

★ The male great bustard is one of the world's heaviest flying birds. It can weigh up to 18 kg (40 lb) and is up to 1 m (3 ft) long.

FEEDING CRANE

Cranes eat a variety of foods, using their strong beaks to catch insects and other small creatures and to pick up seeds and leaves. They often wade into shallow water to find food, but they do not have webbed feet.

Sunbittern displaying its bright feathers

Trumpeter

PUTTING ON A DISPLAY

The sunbittern often stays hidden among shady plants searching for food. However, if alarmed it spreads its wings and shows its brightly colored feathers to scare off its enemy.

TRUMPETER BIRD

Flocks of trumpeters feed together on the forest floor. Their wings are weak, and they rarely fly. They make loud booming calls.

FIND OUT MORE
ATLAS OF THE WORLD: South America
PLANT LIFE: Rushes

Feathers and Flight

All birds have feathers – they are the only creatures that do. Feathers are light and strong, and a bird has different types, each with different jobs to do. Some help the bird to fly and balance in the air, some provide warmth, and others are useful in display.

A bird is able to fly because of the long, strong feathers on its wings and tail. The wing feathers are made up of primary and secondary flight feathers. The primary feathers act as propellers to push the bird along, and the secondaries give lift. To flap its wings, a bird uses its strong chest muscles. The flapping action pushes air back and down, lifting the bird up and along.

WING SHAPES AND FLIGHT

Birds of prey, such as eagles, have large wings with deep slots near the tips of the primary feathers. These slotted feathers help them soar on rising currents of air as they search for food. Seabirds, such as albatrosses, have long, slender wings for flying long distances. Smaller, fast-moving birds, such as swifts, have slim, swept-back wings to help them fly quickly.

An albatross can fly up to 500 km (300 miles) in a day

Albatross

Long, slender wings *allow the bird to glide long distances without flapping its wings*

Bird's wing

Large primary *flight feathers*

Smaller *secondary flight feathers*

Richard's pipit

IN FLIGHT

1 **In normal flight, the** down beat of the wings provides the power to move the bird forward.

Slim, swept-back *wings*

The agile swift *can fly fast and change direction quickly*

Swift

Flight feather

Different types of feathers

Plume *feather*

Down *feather*

TYPES OF FEATHERS

Small, soft down feathers keep a bird warm. Down feathers usually lie beneath the larger feathers. Flight feathers are the biggest, strongest feathers. Many birds also have decorative plume feathers in unusual shapes, which may be used in displays to attract females.

Slots in the *primary feathers help birds of prey to soar*

Large wings *make the eagle a powerful flier*

Eagle

4 **The wings are** at their highest point and ready to begin the down beat again.

2 **During the down beat** the wing feathers spread out to increase the area pushing against the air.

3 **As the wings start** to come up again, the feathers close together to reduce air resistance.

FIND OUT MORE
HUMAN BODY: Muscles
INSIDE MACHINES: Lift

17

Shore Birds

👉 Birds such as avocets, sandpipers, and oystercatchers spend much of their lives in coastal areas and around river mouths and the edges of lakes. Their beaks are specially shaped to help them find the food they eat. They use their beaks to dig small creatures from the mud or to pry shellfish from seashore rocks. Many have long legs and can wade in shallow water as they feed.

BUSY EXPLORING

The dunlin, a kind of sandpiper, is a busy little bird. It pokes about in the mud with its beak as it explores shores or shallow water for food such as worms, snails, or shellfish. Huge flocks of dunlins may gather in areas where there is plenty to eat.

Dunlin walking the shore in search of food

Oystercatcher searching the shore for shellfish

SHELLFISH-EATER

The oystercatcher uses its long, blunt beak to lever oysters and other shellfish off rocks and to pry the strong shells open. It also flies inland to find insects and worms on farmland. There are oystercatchers in most parts of the world.

CURVED BEAK

The avocet has long legs and elegant black and white feathers. It has a very unusual beak that curves upward at the end. The bird sweeps its slender beak from side to side in shallow water or soft mud to find worms and shrimp to eat.

Gulls watching for food on the shore

Curved beak

Long legs
*for wading
in shallow
water*

Avocet

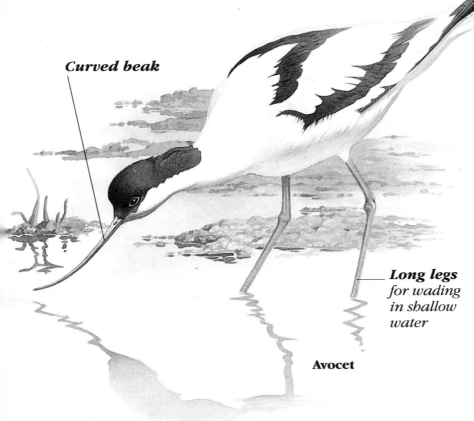

NOISY GULLS

Gulls are large, sturdy birds with long wings and webbed feet. Noisy flocks feed along the edge of the waves, catching small prey. They also steal eggs from other birds' nests and fly inland to find food on farmland and among garbage.

Jacana

AMAZING FACTS

★ Gulls sometimes pick shellfish up and drop them from a height to smash the hard shells open.

★ One shore bird, the golden plover, migrates up to 13,200 km (8,200 miles). It flies between northern North America and South America where it spends the southern summer.

LONG-TOED BIRD

The jacana has toes that are up to 8 cm (3 in) long. These long toes spread the bird's weight over a large area, so that it can walk on floating leaves such as lily pads as it searches for snails, plants, and other food.

FIND OUT MORE
ANIMALS OF THE SEA: Mollusks
PLANT LIFE: Water lilies

Freshwater Birds

Freshwater lakes, ponds, and rivers attract a huge variety of birds. There is plenty of food for them to eat, and many also nest and shelter on the banks. Some freshwater birds, such as flamingos and herons, have long legs and necks and specially shaped beaks, so that they can catch their food as they wade in the water. Birds such as ducks, geese, and swans have webbed feet that push them through the water.

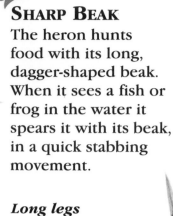

SHARP BEAK
The heron hunts food with its long, dagger-shaped beak. When it sees a fish or frog in the water it spears it with its beak, in a quick stabbing movement.

Long legs *for wading through water*

Gray heron

Stork's nest on a roof top

POWERFUL SWIMMERS
Swans are long-necked birds with all-white or white and black feathers. They can be up to 1.5 m (5 ft) tall. Although swans are powerful swimmers and good fliers, they have short legs and do not walk easily on land.

Swans feed mostly *on water plants*

Tundra swan

CHIMNEY NESTER
Storks are big birds, up to 1 m (3 ft) tall, that fly with their long legs and necks stretched out. They generally nest in groups in trees or even on chimneys at the tops of buildings. The nests are made of sticks.

AMAZING FACTS

★ The whistling swan has 25,216 feathers – the most of any bird whose feathers have been counted.

★ The marabou stork has one of the largest wingspans of any land bird. It measures 3.2 m (10½ ft).

Male mandarin duck

Beak is held upside down
in the water as the bird feeds

BRISTLY BEAK

The flamingo is a tall water bird, up to 1.5 m (5 ft) high. It has an unusual beak that is lined with bristles. As the flamingo feeds, water is taken into the beak and flows out again at the sides, leaving any small creatures and water plants trapped on the bristles.

Long legs allow
flamingo to feed in deeper water than other wading birds

Pink color is
because of the shrimp the bird eats

Water is filtered
through bristles in the beak to trap food

Flamingos wading in water

COURTSHIP SAILS

The very colorful male mandarin duck finds food on the surface of the water. It has feathers on its sides that look like sails and are used in its courtship display. These ducks come from Asia, but have been taken to lakes and ponds all over the world.

FIND OUT MORE
PLANET EARTH: Rivers
REPTILES AND AMPHIBIANS: Frogs

Seabirds

Albatrosses and gannets are some of the many birds that depend on the sea for food. Like most seabirds, they are strong fliers and can soar for hours over the open sea, searching for fish. In fact, some seabirds only come to land to lay eggs and rear young. Most seabirds swim well, and some dive under the water to chase their prey.

MIDAIR PIRATES

Frigate birds are large and strong, with big, hooked beaks. They either snatch food from the water or rob other birds of their food. A frigate bird chases another bird that has a fish and bothers it until it drops or coughs up its catch.

Frigate bird

Forked tail and narrow wings make the frigate bird agile in the air

Shiny, black feathers

Cormorant drying its wings

UNDERWATER DIVERS

The cormorant catches fish by diving under water and chasing its prey. It brings its catch to the surface before eating it. The cormorant's feathers are not completely waterproof, so after a dive it may sit on rocks with its wings spread out to dry.

The albatross has the longest wings of any bird. When fully spread, they measure 3.5 m (11 ft) from tip to tip

LIFE IN THE AIR

The wandering albatross spends most of its life in the air, but it does settle on the sea briefly to snatch squid or fish from just beneath the surface. It also lands on islands near Antarctica to lay its eggs and care for its young.

ANTARCTIC PENGUINS
Penguins cannot fly, but are expert swimmers and divers. They live in the southern hemisphere. Antarctic penguins have a thick layer of fat beneath their feathers to protect them from the freezing waters.

Emperor penguin keeping chick warm

Hooked beak

Tern

Frigate birds chase other birds to make them drop their food

Fish in tern's beak

Pouch for scooping up fish

Pelican

FISHING POUCH
The pelican's long beak has a stretchy pouch of skin below it, which the bird uses as a scoop to catch fish. Several pelicans swim together, herding the fish into a group. Each pelican then fills its pouch with a mouthful of fish.

AMAZING FACTS
★ Huge groups of over 200,000 gannets gather to nest on rocks. Each nesting pair of gannets has to defend its patch of rock, but the birds seem to breed better in these crowded conditions.

Cliff-edge gannet colony

FIND OUT MORE
ANIMALS OF THE SEA: Squid
ATLAS OF THE WORLD: Antarctic

Finding a Mate

When it is time to breed and lay eggs, birds must look for a partner. Finding a mate is not always easy, and male birds have different ways of getting the attention of females.

Some birds, such as thrushes, simply sit on a bush and sing their tuneful songs to attract a female. Others, such as puffins and birds of paradise, have colorful beaks or beautiful feathers. They show off their colors to the plainer females. Some males perform special group displays, stamping and calling while females watch them. Swans and penguins are among the birds that stay together for life once they have found a partner. Other birds find a new mate every year.

Female has plainer plumage

Raggiana birds of paradise

SPLENDID DISPLAY

Birds of paradise are very colorful birds. The Raggiana bird of paradise lives in the forests of New Guinea. The male shows off his splendid feathers in display. He moves his wings up to touch over his back, and lifts the long red feathers at his sides while making high-pitched calls.

Male black grouse displaying

Two thicker plumes extend from the tail

The male puffin's beak is extra colorful when he is trying to attract a mate

GROUP DISPLAY

Groups of male black grouse gather in special areas to display their fine feathers to watching females. They raise and fan out their tails, puff up the red skin flaps beside their eyes, and strut back and forth.

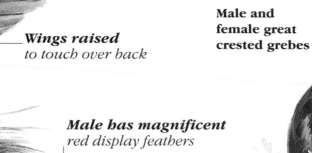

Male and female great crested grebes

Wings raised
to touch over back

Male has magnificent
red display feathers

DANCING GREBES

Male and female great crested grebes perform a series of movements like a dance before they start to nest. During the dance, they offer each other pieces of waterweed.

TASTY GIFT

The male bee-eater brings a present of a freshly caught bee to the female he is courting. This gift encourages the female to trust the male and allow him to come near her.

Male bee-eater

FIND OUT MORE
INSECTS AND SPIDERS: Bees
PLANT LIFE: Pondweed

Birds of Prey

Birds of prey are sharp-eyed hunters and strong fliers. They soar high above the land as they search for food. Their feet have long, sharp claws for catching and killing prey, and they all have strong, hooked beaks for tearing at flesh as they eat. Vultures are slightly different from other birds of prey. They do not usually kill prey, but search for animals that have died or been left by other hunters.

HOVERING HUNTER

The kestrel hovers as it watches for prey – it beats its wings rapidly to keep itself in the same position in the air. When the kestrel spies its prey, such as a mouse, it drops down to catch it in its feet.

Wings beat
very fast

Kestrel

Tail fans out
while hovering

King vulture

Broad wings
for soaring for
long periods

Golden eagle

SMELLING OUT CARRION

The king vulture has no feathers on its head, but its bare skin is brightly colored. Unlike most birds, king vultures have a good sense of smell, which helps them find carrion, or dead animals, to eat.

FLYING HIGH

A superb flier, the golden eagle soars for hours over land as it hunts for food. Mammals, such as hares and rabbits, are its main prey, but it also catches small birds. The eagle kills prey by crushing it with its strong claws.

AMAZING FACTS

★ The bald eagle makes one of the largest of all nests. The nest is up to 2.5 m (8 ft) wide and 6 m (20 ft) deep.

★ The world's biggest eagle is the harpy eagle of South America. It weighs nearly 10 kg (22 lb) and it kills monkeys and porcupines.

Peregrine falcons are expert at flying and hunting

FAST FLIER

The peregrine falcon is one of the fastest fliers. It hunts in the air, making a high-speed dive toward another bird, often a pigeon or dove, and striking it with its feet. As it dives, the falcon may move at more than 180 km/h (110 mph).

Hooked beak

Strong *clawed feet*

Tawny owl swooping down on prey

HUNTING AT NIGHT

Like many other owls, the tawny owl hunts at night. It has amazingly good hearing and large eyes that help it find prey, such as a rat, mouse, or small bird, in poor light.

FIND OUT MORE
MAMMALS: Porcupines
SCIENCE ALL AROUND US: Night vision

27

Pigeons, Parrots, and Cuckoos

Although pigeons, parrots, and cuckoos make up three very different families of birds, they nearly all live in trees. They perch and nest among the branches and find much of their food here as well. Parrots and pigeons eat seeds, nuts, and fruit. Cuckoos also eat insects, which they find on leaves and tree trunks. Most parrots live in the southern half of the world. Pigeons and cuckoos live all over the world.

CHATTERING PARROTS
Noisy groups of eclectus parrots flutter through the trees, feeding on nuts and fruit. In the evening, they perform special display flights before settling down for the night in groups of up to 80 birds.

Female bird *is crimson with a blue belly*

Strong, hooked beak *for holding onto branches and cracking nuts*

Claws hold nut *while bird cracks it open with beak*

Scarlet macaw

STRONG BEAK AND FEET
The scarlet macaw, like all parrots, has strong feet, which it uses for holding food as well as for clinging to branches. The short, hooked beak is extremely powerful and can crack the shells of the hardest nuts.

AMAZING FACTS
★ The greater roadrunner is a type of cuckoo. It can fly but prefers to race along the ground at speeds of up to 20 km/h (12 mph).

★ The largest parrot in the world is the rare, flightless kakapo of New Zealand. Fewer than 60 kakapos now remain.

Yellow-legged pigeon eating a berry

FEEDING PIGEONS

Pigeons sit in trees and eat berries and fruit, but they also pick up scraps of human food. Pigeons are the only birds that produce a creamy liquid, known as pigeon milk, which they feed to their young for a few days after hatching. The milk is made in the throat.

Eclectus parrots in tree

Foster parent with its hungry cuckoo chick

ANOTHER CHICK IN THE NEST

Some types of cuckoos lay their eggs in another bird's nest. When the cuckoo egg hatches, the foster parent struggles to feed a greedy chick that may quickly grow larger than itself.

Male bird has *bright green feathers with blue and red patches*

FIND OUT MORE
MAMMALS: Milk
PLANT LIFE: Fruit

Hornbills and their Relatives

☞ Hornbills, rollers, motmots, and kingfishers may look very different, but they belong to the same group of birds. Most of these birds live and nest in trees, and are very brightly colored or have striking black and white feathers. Insects and small creatures, such as frogs and lizards, are their main foods, but hornbills and motmots also eat fruit, and some kingfishers eat fish. Quetzals belong to a different group, but like hornbills, they nest in tree holes, and eat fruit and insects.

NESTING INSIDE A TREE
The female hornbill lays her eggs in a hole in a tree. The male then helps wall up the nest with mud, leaving a small opening to pass food through. The female stays there, safe from enemies, keeping her eggs warm until they hatch.

Male's beak is 30 cm (12 in) long, just the right shape for passing food through the slit

Great Indian hornbills

SWINGING TAIL
The brightly colored motmot has long tail feathers with tips shaped like spoons. The bird swings its tail from side to side as it sits on a branch watching for prey such as insects or lizards.

Motmot

AMAZING FACT
★ At one hornbill nest, the male bird brought about 24,000 pieces of fruit during the nesting period.

DIVING THROUGH THE AIR
The roller usually perches on a low branch, watching for prey such as insects and other small creatures. It then dives to catch its food on the ground or in midair.

Roller

Nesting female has to rely on the male hornbill to bring her food

RIVERSIDE HUNTER
The kingfisher does not actually swim, but it dives from a riverside perch to snatch prey from the water with its large beak. Many kingfishers also hunt on land, catching insects and lizards.

Kingfisher diving to catch a small fish

Nest built inside tree

Male quetzal

Tail feathers are shed after each mating season, but grow again

COLORFUL TAIL FEATHERS
The male quetzal has bright green tail feathers, which may be up to 1 m (3 ft) long. It flutters these feathers as it makes special display flights to attract females.

FIND OUT MORE
MAMMALS: Burrows
REPTILES AND AMPHIBIANS: Lizards

Nest Building

Birds build nests to lay their eggs in. Nests help to keep the eggs warm and safe from egg-eating animals until the young birds hatch. The way a bird builds its nest depends on where it lives.

Some woodland birds build nests of twigs and leaves high in the trees or in plants close to the ground. Others weave nests that hang from branches. Woodpeckers nest in holes in trees, which they make with their strong beaks. Seabirds, such as guillemots, lay their eggs on a rocky ledge or cliff. This still offers protection because it is hard for enemies to reach the eggs. A few birds dig burrows in the ground, and some use nest boxes built by humans.

Small birds, such as tits, are happy to make a nest box their home

Small opening near the top of the nest allows the bird to get in and out

Penduline tit and its nest

Parent bird bringing food to the chicks

WOVEN NEST
The little penduline tit makes a neat nest like a small bag that hangs from a twig. The nest is woven from plants and animal hair, such as sheep's wool. It has an entrance on one side. The eggs, and later the baby birds, are safely hidden inside.

Nest is made from leaves, grasses, and animal hair

NEST IN THE GROUND
The burrowing owl of North America lays its eggs in a hole in the ground. It may use a hole left by a prairie dog or other animal, but can also dig its own burrow, using its beak and strong feet.

Burrowing owls

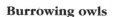

STICKY NEST

Swifts make their nests on cliffs, cave walls, or even on buildings. The nest is made of leaves, stems, and feathers stuck together with sticky saliva, or spit, from the bird's mouth.

Swift nests inside a cave

Guillemots nesting on a cliff ledge

CLIFF-LEDGE NEST

The guillemot lays a single egg on a bare cliff ledge by the sea. The egg may look as if it could easily roll off the ledge, but it is pointed at one end and so rolls in a circle if touched.

NEST OVER WATER

The coot makes a nest that floats on the water and is attached to reeds or other water plants. The male bird brings material such as dead leaves and stems, and the female builds the nest.

Coots on their nest

FIND OUT MORE
PLANET EARTH: Caves
HUMAN BODY: Saliva

33

Woodland and Forest Birds

Toucans and their relatives all spend their lives in and around trees and make their nests in tree holes. Most have strong feet for holding onto branches and tree trunks. Their wings are short and rounded for flying among trees and their beaks are strong. Jacamars and honeyguides feed mainly on insects, but most of these birds eat both fruit and insects.

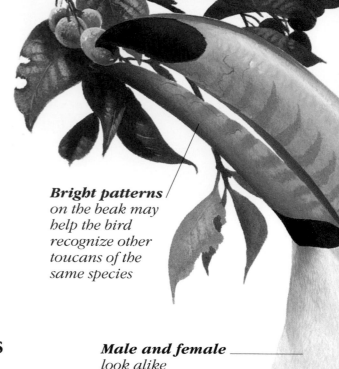

Bright patterns on the beak may help the bird recognize other toucans of the same species

Male and female look alike

Jacamar in flight

LONG-BEAKED TOUCAN

The toucan's long, colorful beak helps it to reach fruit at the end of branches that are too thin to take its weight. The bird picks the fruit with the tip of its beak, then tosses the fruit back into its mouth.

Toco toucan

HUNTING IN THE AIR

A small bird with glittering feathers, the jacamar darts out from a perch to catch flying insects such as butterflies or dragonflies. It seizes its prey in its long, sharp beak and returns to its perch to eat its catch.

Double-toothed barbet

TREE-LIVING BARBET
The plump little barbet has a large head and a sturdy beak fringed with bristles. It is not a powerful flier and spends most of its life in trees. It climbs well with the help of its strong legs and feet.

Woodpecker has long, sharp claws for clinging to tree trunks

AMAZING FACTS

★ Woodpeckers keep in touch with each other by drumming on tree trunks with their beaks.

★ The honeyguide is able to eat and digest bees' waxy honeycomb as well as the bee larvae.

PECKING AWAY
The woodpecker clings to a tree trunk and hammers at the bark with its sharp beak. Its stiff tail feathers help to support its body. Once it has made a hole, the bird uses its long tongue to pick out insects and small spiders beneath the bark.

HELPFUL HONEYGUIDES
The honeyguide likes to eat young bee grubs, or larvae, but needs help breaking into a bees' nest. It calls and flicks its tail to attract the attention of a honey badger or human, both of which love honey. The bird shows its "helper" the nest and waits while it is broken open.

Honeyguide and honey badger

Short wings *mean that the toucan cannot fly well*

Strong *claws*

FIND OUT MORE
INSECTS AND SPIDERS: Butterflies
PLANET EARTH: Forests

Feeding on the Wing

👉 **M**any birds catch food in the air and return to their perch to eat it. Swifts, hummingbirds, and nightjars are special because they catch and eat their food as they fly. In fact, swifts do almost everything, except laying eggs and caring for young, while flying. To feed, they fly with their mouths open, taking in insects as they go. Hummingbirds are also experts in the air, but they hover as they feed – they beat their wings very fast to keep them still in the air as they sip nectar, a sweet liquid, from flowers.

DARTING HERE AND THERE
The amazing swift darts through the air, rarely coming to land. It even sleeps as it flies. Its legs and feet are weak, making it awkward on the ground.

Long feathers on the outside, short on the inside, give the wing its curved shape

Eurasian swift

Wide-open mouth for catching insects in the air

Nightjar

NIGHT FLIER
The nightjar flies close to the ground with its mouth open, scooping up night-flying insects, such as moths. The bristles on the beak help trap prey. In the day, the bird roosts on the ground or in trees, where its brownish feathers help keep it hidden.

AMAZING FACTS
★ Once a young swift leaves its nest, it may not land again until it first breeds, two years later. By this time, it may have flown 500,000 km (300,000 miles) without stopping.

Curved beak

White-tipped sicklebill hummingbird

CAVE DWELLER
The oilbird, a relative of the nightjar, lives in caves. It flies out at night to eat the oily fruits of palm trees, which it picks in mid flight. It stores the fruits in its stomach and digests them next day.

Oilbird in its cave

HOVERING BIRDS
Tiny, colorful hummingbirds can fly in any direction as well as hover. Their beaks are shaped to suit the flowers they feed from. The sicklebill's curved beak is ideal for bell-shaped flowers. The sword-billed hummingbird feeds from deep, trumpet-shaped flowers.

Sword-billed hummingbird

Beak is 12 cm (4¾ in) long

Forked tail

Hummingbird measures only 7.5 cm (3 in) from head to tail

Long, thin wings allow the swift to dart through the air

HARD TO SPOT
The tawny frogmouth is a relative of the nightjar. By day, it rests on a branch, where its grayish-brown feathers make it hard to see against the bark. At night it eats insects and hunts small creatures, such as mice.

Frogmouth

FIND OUT MORE
INSECTS AND SPIDERS: Moths
PLANT LIFE: Nectar

Broadbills and their Relatives

Most broadbills and their relatives live in warm, southern parts of the world. Broadbills, pittas, and antbirds all eat insects and other small creatures, which they find on the ground. Tyrant flycatchers eat insects, too, but they often catch their prey in the air. Two particularly attractive birds in this group are the cock of the rock and the lyrebird. Both have amazing feathers, which they display to attract females.

SCISSOR-TAILED FLYCATCHER

In flight, the long, graceful tail feathers of the tyrant flycatcher open and close like a pair of scissors. During his courtship flight, the male bird tumbles and somersaults, with his tail feathers twisting like ribbons.

Tyrant flycatcher

Broad beak *for catching insects in the air*

White-plumed antbird

FOLLOWING ANTS

The little antbird follows groups of army ants as they march through the jungle. It does not catch the ants themselves, but it perches just above the ground to snap up other insects as they escape the approaching army.

Tail feathers
*are up to 60 cm
(24 in) long*

NEST WEAVER

The broadbill lives in forests and
woodland. Its oval-shaped nest is
woven from plant fibers and hangs
from a low branch, often close to
or over a stream.

**Broadbill with
hanging nest**

Tail feathers
*are about 23 cm
(9 in) long*

Male lyrebird

DANCING DISPLAY

The Australian lyrebird has plain
brownish feathers, but the male
has a beautiful tail. Some of the long
tail feathers are extremely fine, while
others have a curving shape. Before
mating, the male bird dances in
front of the female, spreading his
glorious tail over his body.

Cock of the rock

BRIGHT ORANGE DISPLAY

The brightly colored male
cock of the rock lives in South
American forests. The large
crest of feathers on the bird's
head curves down onto his
beak. Groups of male birds
perform displays to show off
their feathers to females.

AMAZING FACTS

★ Some broadbills make
a noise with their beating
wings that can carry
across distances of up to
60 m (200 ft). The sound
may help to warn other
birds off their territory.

Banded pitta

SEARCHING IN THE LEAVES

Pittas are plump birds with strong
beaks and short tails. Most live
on or near the ground in African
and Asian forests, where they
search among the leaves for
insects and other small creatures.

FIND OUT MORE
INSECTS AND SPIDERS: Army ants
PLANET EARTH: Rain forests

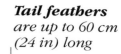
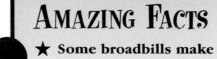

Eggs and Young

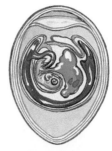

All birds lay eggs from which their young hatch. Unlike mammals, birds do not carry their developing young inside their bodies. The extra weight would make the birds too heavy to fly.

The hard shell of the egg protects the baby bird as it develops, and the yolk inside the egg provides it with food. The parent birds must incubate the egg, or keep it warm, while the baby inside grows. Most birds do this by sitting on the eggs in a nest and keeping them warm with their own body heat. When a chick is ready to hatch, it makes its own way out of the egg. Most chicks have a special egg tooth – a hard spike on the beak that is used to break the shell.

EMBRYO DEVELOPMENT

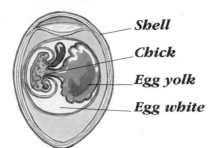

Shell
Chick
Egg yolk
Egg white

1 Developing chick is protected by the layers of egg white as well as by the shell.

2 As the chick grows, it feeds on the yolk. Air reaches the chick through the shell.

Parent blackbird brings a worm to its chicks

Chicks with wide-open beaks, begging for food

Female blackbird feeding its chicks

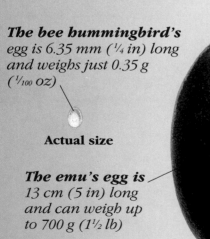

The bee hummingbird's egg is 6.35 mm (¼ in) long and weighs just 0.35 g (¹⁄₁₀₀ oz)

Actual size

The emu's egg is 13 cm (5 in) long and can weigh up to 700 g (1½ lb)

HELPLESS CHICKS

A blackbird chick cannot even lift its head when it first hatches. It is looked after by both parents, which regularly bring it food. The chick grows quickly and after two or three weeks, it will learn to fly.

Half size

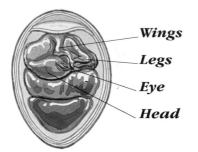

Wings
Legs
Eye
Head

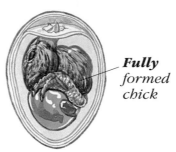

Fully formed chick

Cygnets stay close to their mother until grown

3 The chick now has a large head and eyes, and its legs and wings are forming.

4 Now the chick is ready to break out of the shell and finish growing outside the egg.

Parent brings food to its young for up to 19 days

Adult bird uses its beak to turn the eggs and warm them evenly

FENDING FOR THEMSELVES

Young swans, called cygnets, are able to swim with their parents and find food for themselves. But the parents do protect the cygnets. Mute swans carry their young on their backs when they become tired or frightened.

FOLLOWING MOTHER

Some young birds, such as ducklings, automatically follow the first moving thing they see after hatching. This is usually the mother, which means that the birds will stay close to their parents and out of danger. But if a duckling saw a person when it first hatched, it would follow that person instead.

WARMING THE EGGS

Both the male and female reed warbler take it in turns to keep their eggs warm. They sit on them for a total of 11 or 12 days until the chicks are ready to hatch.

Reed warbler incubating its eggs

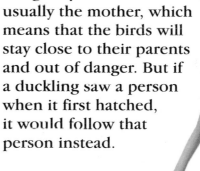

FIND OUT MORE
HUMAN BODY: Growing up
MAMMALS: Babies

Singing and Perching

Almost half of all species of bird belong to a large group known as songbirds. Most male songbirds can sing musical sequences of notes when courting females or defending their territory, the area in which they live. Songbirds are also called perching birds. They have four toes, three pointing forward and one backward, which are ideally shaped for holding onto perches such as branches or even wires. Not all songbirds feed in trees. Larks and pipits usually find their food on the ground, and swallows catch insects in the air.

NOISY BULBULS
Chattering flocks of bulbuls land in fruit trees in forests, or even gardens, and can damage crops. They also search the ground to find insects, such as ants. Male and female birds look alike.

Red-whiskered bulbuls in tree

Short, slightly *curved beak*

Young swallows stay in the nest being fed by their parents for up to 24 days

Male and female birds look similar, but the male has longer tail feathers

Barn swallows

NESTING SWALLOW
The barn swallow makes a rough nest of mud and plants. It attaches the nest to the wall of a cave or even a barn or other type of building. Barn swallows live worldwide.

NODDING HEADS

All pipits nod their heads up and down and wag their tails from side to side as they walk. The water pipit wades into shallow water or mud to catch water insects and worms.

Pipit ready to catch insects

Skylark

SONG FLIGHT

Many birds sing while sitting on a perch, but the skylark sings its tuneful song while in flight. It flutters and hovers high in the sky for long periods, singing the whole time.

Body is 20 cm (8 in) long

Red feathers near the ears

SINGING MIMIC

The mockingbird has its own song, which it sings night and day. It is also well known as an expert at imitating the songs of other birds or even cars, sirens, and barking dogs.

Mockingbird

AMAZING FACTS

★ Young swallows eat 400 meals a day. Their parents are kept busy bringing them a constant supply of insects.

FIND OUT MORE
DANCE, DRAMA, AND MUSIC: Singers
INSECTS AND SPIDERS: Worms

Insect-eating Songbirds

☞**M**any songbirds, such as flycatchers, are very good at catching insects. Most flycatchers have specially bristled or broad, slightly hooked beaks, which they use to snatch insects from the air. Not all of these insect-eating songbirds are good singers, however. Unlike warblers and thrushes, babblers are not known for their beautiful songs. Instead, they usually communicate with noisy chattering as they feed.

DARTING FLYCATCHER
The red-breasted flycatcher spends the spring and summer in forests and woodlands in Eastern Europe and central Asia, where it lays its eggs and rears its young. It then flies south to warmer areas for the rest of the year.

Adult male

Red-breasted flycatchers

Golden-headed fantail warbler at its nest

SMALL WARBLER
The golden-headed fantail warbler spends most of its time on the ground, looking for insects. Its nest is made of grass and spiders' webs and is hidden among long grass. The nest's entrance is at the top.

AMAZING FACTS

★ The grasshopper warbler sings a high-pitched song, making up to 1,400 triple notes in a minute.

★ The marsh warbler can imitate the songs of more than 70 other kinds of birds.

Juvenile, or young bird, has not yet developed adult markings

Pale brown throat and breast

Yellow-eyed babbler

NEAT NEST BUILDERS

Calling constantly, pairs or small groups of yellow-eyed babblers search for insects to eat. These birds make a neat nest of grass and strips of bark, covered with spiders' webs.

Wide beak with bristles to help trap prey in the air

Insect prey, which adult darts out to catch

Red throat and breast

Whistling thrush

WHISTLING ALARM

The whistling thrush of Asia makes a loud, whistling alarm call, as well as a more musical song. It lives in forested mountain areas, often close to streams.

FIND OUT MORE
INSECTS AND SPIDERS: Spiders' webs
MAMMALS: Insect-eaters

45

Tree-living Songbirds

☞**M**any songbirds find shelter and food in trees. They do not need to be powerful fliers and simply flit from tree to tree, picking up insects and fruit in their pointed beaks. Their strong feet and claws help them hold onto branches and tree trunks. The colorful sunbird eats some insects, but it also takes nectar from flowers. It plunges its long, curved beak deep inside the flower to feed.

ACTIVE FLOWERPECKER

Only about 9 cm (3½ in) long, the scarlet-backed flowerpecker is a noisy, active little bird. It darts around flowers, seizing insects and berries or sipping nectar.

Scarlet-backed flowerpecker

Short legs *and tail*

Japanese white-eye

SIPPING NECTAR

The Japanese white-eye uses its beak to take insects from bark and pick spiders off leaves. It also sips nectar from flowers with its brush-tipped tongue. White-eyes move in small flocks, keeping in touch with quiet trilling calls.

Caciques feed, nest, and roost in groups

HANGING NEST

Groups of South American caciques roost near one another in trees. Each pair makes an amazing baglike nest, woven from grass and other plants, which hangs from a branch. Staying together helps protect the birds' eggs and young from hungry enemies.

Long, tube-shaped *tongue for feeding on flower nectar*

Male fire-tailed sunbird

Strong feet *for clinging to branch while feeding*

Nuthatches hop *up and down trees in search of insects*

Nuthatch

COLORFUL SUNBIRD

Only the male fire-tailed sunbird has brilliant red, yellow, and blue feathers. The smaller female bird is grayish-brown. Sunbirds usually perch near a flower while they take nectar.

CLIMBING BIRDS

Nuthatches and creepers have strong legs and sharp claws to help them cling to bark as they feed. Their pointed beaks are just the right shape for poking into cracks in tree trunks to find insects to eat.

Wallcreepers *flick their wings as they search for insects to eat*

Wallcreeper

AMAZING FACTS

★ The little blue tit is only 11 cm (4¼ in) long, but it lays as many as 15 eggs at a time. This is more than any other bird that feeds its young.

Blue tit with nest full of eggs

FIND OUT MORE
HUMAN BODY: Tongue
PLANT LIFE: Flowers

Seed-eating Songbirds

Seeds of all kinds are important foods for many songbirds. Birds such as finches and buntings have strong, often cone-shaped, beaks for crushing hard seeds and removing the husk, or tough outer covering. The shape of the beak varies according to the type of seed the bird normally eats. Those that eat the largest seeds have beaks almost like a parrot's. Many of these birds also catch insects for themselves and to feed to their young.

CROSSED-OVER BEAK

The red crossbill is a little finch with an unusual beak – the upper and lower parts cross over at the tips. The bird uses its beak to open tough pine cones and take the seeds out.

Only the male red crossbill is red; females are greenish-gray

Male zebra finch

Chest stripes and bright patches on face

FLOCKS OF ZEBRAS

Zebra finches are common Australian birds that move in large flocks of up to 100 birds. They often nest in groups, too, each pair making a dome-shaped nest of grass and twigs in a tree or bush.

AMAZING FACTS

★ The snow bunting nests in the Arctic, farther north than any other bird. It even burrows into the snow to escape the cold air.

Tanager

TREE-LIVING TANAGER

Tanagers spend most of their lives in trees eating fruit and seeds, as well as snapping up any insects they can find. They make cup-shaped nests on branches.

NEST WEAVER

The male baya weaver of western Africa makes a rounded nest, which hangs from a branch or wire. The nest is carefully woven from grass and other plants and has an entrance at the bottom. Each male may have several mates and builds a nest for each one.

Male baya weaver on a nest

Male red crossbill taking seeds from a cone

Beak crosses over at tips

Scales of the cone held open while the tongue takes the seeds out

Pine bunting

GROUND FEEDERS

Buntings usually feed on the ground, scratching for seeds with their strong feet or taking seeds from plants with their beaks. They nest on or near the ground, too, in a cup-shaped nest built by the female bird.

Reed bunting

FIND OUT MORE
ATLAS OF THE WORLD: Polar regions
PLANT LIFE: Pine cones

Birds on the Move

Twice a year, many birds take part in amazing journeys called migrations. Most migrating birds spend the spring and summer in the north and fly south in the fall to escape the winter. They return north when the weather there warms up again and so have sunshine and plentiful food all year round.

Migrating birds can travel huge distances and have various methods of finding their way. Birds seem to be born with some knowledge of where to go, because young birds can migrate without adults. Scientists think that they also use the Sun, stars, and familiar landmarks to help them. Most make regular stops to rest and feed.

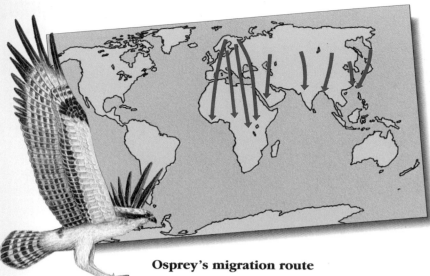

Osprey's migration route

FISH-EATING TRAVELER

A large bird of prey, the osprey flies up to 10,000 km (6,000 miles) on its migration. It is a strong flier, and because its main food is fish, it travels from one large area of water to another, stopping to catch fish as it goes.

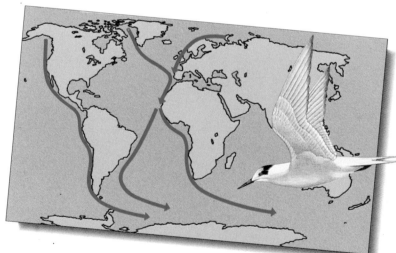

Arctic tern flies from one polar region to the other

FROM TOP TO BOTTOM

The Arctic tern makes the longest migration of any bird. It flies about 20,000 km (12,500 miles) from the Arctic, where it nests, to the Antarctic, where it spends the southern summer.

Humans use detailed maps to find their way

FORMATION FLYING

Large birds such as geese and cranes fly in a V-shaped group when they migrate. Each bird can see the one in front without being affected by the air it disturbs as it flaps its wings.

Geese flying in formation

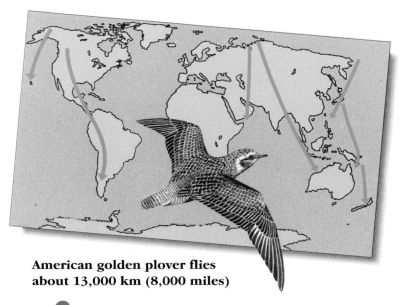

American golden plover flies about 13,000 km (8,000 miles)

NONSTOP JOURNEY

Golden plovers nest in the far north of North America, Siberia, and northern Asia during the summer months. When winter arrives, they migrate south. The American golden plover flies from North to South America without stopping.

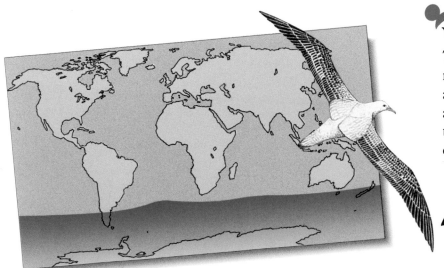

Albatross keeps to the southernmost part of the world

WORLD WANDERER

The wandering albatross does not migrate north to south, but makes a continuous journey around and around the southernmost part of the world. It lands on small islands only to mate and lay eggs.

FIND OUT MORE
ATLAS OF THE WORLD: Polar regions
PLANET EARTH: Seasons

Larger Songbirds

Although most songbirds are small, some, such as crows, grow up to 63 cm (25 in) long. Crows have strong beaks and are powerful hunters. They are thought to be among the most intelligent of all birds. Male and female crows look alike. Male birds of paradise, however, are dramatically different from the much duller females. They use their beautiful feathers in courtship displays to attract mates.

DECORATED BOWER
The male satin bowerbird makes a structure of sticks called an avenue bower to impress the female. He paints it with a paste of chewed fruit and adds pieces of decoration. These may be flowers, berries, or even bottle-tops, and are nearly always blue.

Male bird has dark, glossy feathers

Satin bowerbirds

Racket-tailed drongo

UNUSUAL TAIL FEATHERS
The racket-tailed drongo has a crest on its head and tail feathers that measure up to 35 cm (14 in) long. A noisy bird, it catches insects in the air and searches branches and leaves for food.

Racket-shaped tips to tail feathers

AMAZING FACTS
★ Scientists believe that ravens, the largest type of crow, can count. Some birds have counted up to five or six in experiments.

THIEVING MAGPIE
The magpie is a type of crow and will eat almost anything it can find. It steals the eggs and young of other birds from their nests, but also catches pests, such as rats and mice.

Magpie

UPSIDE-DOWN DISPLAY

The brilliantly colored male blue bird of paradise displays his feathers by hanging upside down. He then swings his long tail streamers to and fro in front of the watching female.

Male blue bird of paradise

Male golden oriole feeding a grub to its young

TUNEFUL SONG

Like all orioles, the golden oriole has a beautiful, tuneful call. It weaves its nest from grass and hangs it between two twigs, like a hammock. The nest is built by the female bird. The male helps the female care for the young.

Curving walls
of bower are about 10 cm (4 in) apart

Male builds
a bower to attract females

Female makes
a separate nest in which she lays her eggs

FIND OUT MORE
HUMAN BODY: Voice
MAMMALS: Rats

Birds in Today's World

Birds the world over are in danger. More than 1,000 of the 9,000 species are so rare that they could become extinct, or die out forever. Human activities are putting more birds at risk than ever before. Areas where birds live, such as woodlands, lakes, and rivers, are being destroyed or polluted. Birds are often hunted and shot or captured to keep as pets. But we can help save these birds. Some rare birds can be bred in captivity for release into the wild, and we can open nature reserves, where birds will be protected.

A type of vulture, the condor scavenges for animals that are already dead

Condor lays only one egg every two years, so increasing numbers takes a long time

DECREASING NUMBERS

At one time there were only nine California condors left in the wild. But birds have been bred in captivity and in 1997 there were 121 condors, some of which have been released into the wild.

Oil being washed from bird's feathers

CLEANING BEACHES

Oil spills from huge tankers at sea can kill wildlife and pollute the environment. If a bird gets oil on its feathers it cannot fly. When it tries to clean itself, it may swallow so much oil that it dies.

Siberian white crane

HELPING HAND

To help save the Siberian white crane, eggs laid by captive birds are put in the nests of other types of cranes. It is hoped that the new parents will care for the eggs and young with their own, and so help to build up the numbers of wild birds.

AMAZING FACTS

★ Parrots are in more danger of extinction than any other group of birds. Out of 350 species, more than 90 could soon be extinct.

★ Just one cat on a tiny island off New Zealand made a species of wren extinct. In six months it killed every single wren.

FOREST UNDER THREAT

Large areas of the rain forest, home to the monkey-eating Philippine eagle, have been chopped down. This eagle is now one of the world's rarest birds. Large birds of prey like this cannot survive without a big area in which to hunt.

Philippine eagle

A RARE BIRD

So many indigo macaws were trapped for the pet trade that in 1978 there were only 60 left. This bird has also suffered from the destruction of its habitat and food plants, which have been cleared to make farmland.

Indigo macaw

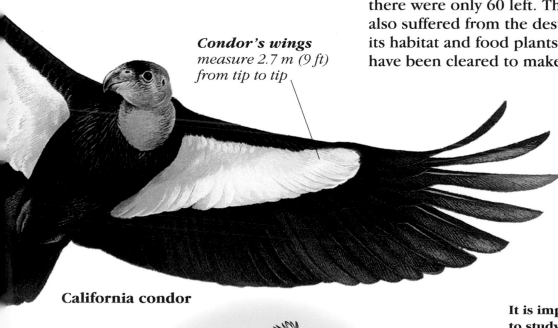

Condor's wings measure 2.7 m (9 ft) from tip to tip

California condor

It is important to study birds so we can help protect them

FIND OUT MORE
DINOSAURS: Extinction
MAMMALS: Conservation

Glossary of Key Words

Air resistance: The force exerted by the air as a bird, for example, moves against it.

Breed: To produce young.

Burrow: An underground hole where an animal makes its nest.

Captivity: Keeping an animal caged or fenced in, such as in a zoo or safari park.

Carrion: The bodies of animals that have died naturally or been killed. Some birds, such as vultures, feed on carrion.

Casque: A bony part on the head or beak of a bird, usually made of horn.

Colony: A large group of birds that live and nest together. Many seabirds, such as gannets and penguins, live in colonies.

Courtship display: A series of movements made to attract mates. Displays are usually performed by males to attract females.

Current: A flow of air or water moving in a certain direction.

Display flight: A special way of flying that is part of a courtship display for attracting mates.

Down: The small, soft feathers that lie beneath a bird's main feathers and help to keep it warm.

Egg tooth: A hard spike on the beak of a baby bird, which helps it break out of the egg. This "tooth" is lost after hatching.

Egg white: The clear substance around the yolk inside an egg that helps protect the developing chick.

Egg yolk: The yellow substance inside an egg that provides food for the growing chick.

Extinction: The process by which all individuals of a species, or particular type, die out.

Flock: A large group of birds flying or feeding together.

Habitat: The natural environment in which an animal lives.

Hatch: To come out of an egg.

Hovering: A special kind of flight when a bird stays in one place in the air, feeding or watching for prey.

Imitate: To copy the sounds or actions of something, for example another bird.

Incubation: The process of keeping eggs warm until they hatch. Birds usually do this by sitting on the eggs and warming them with their own body heat.

Keratin: The material that makes up feathers, claws, beaks, and horns.

Larva: A stage in an insect's life between an egg and an adult.

Mammal: An animal that gives birth to live young and does not usually lay eggs.

Migration: A regular, usually seasonal, journey made by birds, to areas where they breed or find food.

Nature reserve: A protected area of land where plants and animals live and breed in safety.

Nectar: A sweet liquid that is produced by many plants. Both birds and insects feed on nectar.

Nest: A safe place where a bird lays its eggs and rears its young.

Plumage: A bird's covering of feathers.

Polar regions: The areas around the Earth's North and South Poles.

Polluted: Damaged or made dirty by waste materials, such as smoke, fumes, or garbage.

Preening: The process by which a bird uses its beak to clean its feathers of insects and dirt.

Prey: Animals that are hunted and eaten by other animals.

Primary feathers: The large feathers on a bird's wings that help push the bird along during flight.

Rain forest: Thick forest that grows in warm, tropical areas with heavy rainfall all year round.

Rear: To bring up and look after young animals.

Roost: A place where a bird rests or sleeps. A resting bird is said to be roosting.

Savanna: A tropical grassland.

Scavenger: A bird that feeds on garbage or carrion.

Secondary feathers: The short feathers that help to lift a bird during takeoff and flight.

Species: A particular type of animal whose individuals are very similar and can breed together.

Territory: The special area where an animal lives and finds its food.

Tropical: The lands around the Equator where the climate is hot all year round.

Tundra: A vast, flat, treeless plain in Arctic and alpine regions. The ground of the tundra is often frozen.

Waterproof: Able to allow water to run off and remain dry. The oil-coated feathers of birds are usually waterproof.

Index

(*see* **Famous Places** for a full index to your complete set of books)